5/14/68

Gladys — Thanks
for your friendship
and to all the good
things you do around
here!

Pastor Mark Wegener

RITUALS OF REDEMPTION

Sermons On The Meaning
Of Liturgical Ceremonies

BY MARK I. WEGENER

RITUALS OF REDEMPTION

FIRST EDITION
Copyright © 1992 by
Mark Wegener

All scripture quotations are the author's own translations.

7916 / ISBN 1-55673-463-8   PRINTED IN U.S.A.

With thanks to
Elmer and Muriel Jasten,
generous "liturgists"
in the best sense of the word.

Table Of Contents

Introduction

Some church people are becoming more interested in things liturgical. They are discovering that traditional rituals and ceremonies can have great meaning when done carefully in a community that appreciates the historical roots of Christian worship. Perhaps this trend is a reaction to some of the less formal, more casual styles of worship popular in many congregations. Perhaps it is a signal that we are recoving the treasures bequeathed by our ancestors in the faith.

In any event, it is heartening to see Christian men and women taking serious interest in the things they do as they worship. In a sense we have no choice about whether we will use rituals and ceremonies; the only question is *which* rites and liturgies we will employ. Making the sign of the cross, kneeling and bowing, processing for the Gospel, even burning incense — these actions enable us to involve our bodies, and therefore our selves, in our worship. They join more customary actions — such as singing hymns, receiving offerings, and sharing the peace — in enriching our sense of devotion.

Of course, rituals by themselves are worth nothing. If they do not enable worshipers to embody their faith and to respond to the Gospel they can even be hindrances. For there's nothing worse than empty ceremonial for obscuring the intention of true religion. Therefore good liturgy should not become an end in itself but remain as the framework for the preaching of the Gospel and the celebration of the Sacraments.

The members of Mount Olive Lutheran Church in Minneapolis have grown to appreciate the value of liturgical ceremonies for enriching their worship. These sermons were originally preached there during the nine weeks which included the festivals of the Reformation and All Saints and which ended with Christ the King. Each includes two texts, a verse from the psalms plus a New Testament passage. They often include references to our parish's unique practices, which will not apply elsewhere.

Nevertheless I trust these homilies will assist others not only to appreciate the history and symbolism behind these worship practices but more importantly to make connections between liturgy and real life. We have called them "Rituals of Redemption" and pray they will continue to be meaningful expressions of our common faith.

— MIW —

6

Baptism And The Sign Of The Cross

Be thorough at washing me from my iniquity,
and from my sins cleanse me.
— *Psalm 51:2*

And as he came close Jesus spoke to them.
"All authority in heaven and on earth is given
to me," he said. "So as you travel, disciple all
the nations, baptizing them in the name of the
Father and the Son and the Holy Spirit, teach-
ing them to keep everything which I ordered
you. And look, I myself am with you all the
days, until this aeon is completed."
— *Matthew 28:18-20*

This morning we begin a series of nine sermons, all dealing with the meaning and impact of some of the traditional
ceremonies we enjoy as part of our regular worship. These are
the *Rituals of Redemption.* That is, these are the customary
motions we perform, the gestures and stances and movements
we make as we try to get our bodies involved in our worship.
For we experience our redemption as the people of God right
here in our worship. So our rituals in this place are *Rituals*
of Redemption.

A social anthropologist would be happy to explain to us
the importance of the ceremonies and rituals which we perform within a church or temple. One of my books puts it this
way:

A sacred place is a place of clarification (a focusing lens)
where [people] and gods are held to be transparent to one
another.

7

It is a place where static and noise are decreased so that the exchange of information can be increased, [and] the device by which this is accomplished is redundancy, through ritual repetition and routinization. [1]

That's a fancy way of saying that what we do and how we do it really counts, especially when we are in church. Our rituals and ceremonies matter to us because they are the motions of worship and therefore the movements of the God who frees us. They are *Rituals of Redemption.*

And for a congregation like ours ritual is doubly important. For we put so many of our eggs in the liturgical basket. We have a reputation not only in the Twin Cities but in fact throughout the United States for being a parish where, as some have said, "they do worship right." And whether we are called "high church" (which is not always a compliment) or as, I would prefer, "intentionally liturgical," the fact remains that our traditions and ceremonies are important to our worship.

The strange thing is, we seem to enjoy our holy play, our bowing and kneeling and so forth. One of the things I hear in my sophomore high school religion class is the repeated complaint that worship is so "boring." "Everybody is so serious and formal," they say. "Why can't we liven it up?" So I told them about our services, how people turn toward the cross and bow and kneel and cross themselves and so forth. "Yuck," they said, "I'm glad I don't go there. I'd hate to have to do that all the time."

So I answered, "You're wrong. The people do it because they want to, not because they have to. That's how they make their worship interesting. That's how they keep awake. They play by those rules so the game becomes more challenging, more fun, and more meaningful." I don't know whether they bought that; sophomores are hard to convince. But I suspect that most of you who have joined this congregation in the past few years have done so precisely because you are more mature than sophomores, and although you may like your steaks medium-rare you prefer your worship well done.

8

And therein lies the danger. We can get so caught up in performing our worship well that that's all we will have — a nice performance. Jesus had something to say about that, you know. "Beware of practicing your piety before people in order to be seen by them," he warned, "for then you will have no reward from your Father who is in heaven." (Matthew 6:1)

Now the remedy for sterile ritual is not sloppy worship; it is ritual with meaning, ceremony with understanding. So our task these nine weeks is not merely to explain the history of our worship traditions or give directives for how to do it, but to recover the essential meaning of our ceremonies. Furthermore, our business is not only that, but also to go on from meaning to application, to discover how our rituals impact the deep issues of our everyday living. For if we are able to find our lives redeemed, then we will have discovered the *Rituals of Redemption.*

And the first of them is the Sign of the Cross. Most of you know how to do it, even if some of you don't feel comfortable doing it. You use your finger tips to trace the shape of a cross, up and down touching your forehead and your chest, then side to side from shoulder to shoulder.

Most Christians who grew up in the western catholic tradition go from left to right. Others learned the eastern orthodox style from right to left so you end on the side of your heart. Which you prefer matters little. And as you bless yourself with the Sign of the Cross you say either aloud or silently, "In the Name of the Father, and of the Son, and of the Holy Spirit."

By the way, some people have the idea that the motion is an "extra" you can do to supplement the saying of the trinitarian invocation. Actually it is the other way around. In ancient times people made the Sign of the Cross long before somebody decided to add the words.

Now let's be frank. When your friends join you for worship here, many of them will be, well if not shocked, at least mildly surprised to see so many Lutherans making the Sign of the Cross. "I thought only Catholics did that," they will

9

say. And 30 or 40 years ago they would have been right. What they don't realize is that the Sign of the Cross was one of the ceremonies that Luther and the Reformers were intent on keeping.

Apparently it was abandoned in America when immigrants from southern Europe were coming to our shores and Lutherans were determined not to be "like that." It was a time when there was a lot of anti-Catholic prejudice in the land, and a time when our great-great-grandparents were trying like the devil to become more acclimated to mainstream American Protestantism. So the Sign of the Cross was one of the casualties of the battle.

Which is a shame, because we lost something valuable there, something eminently Lutheran. You know, in our *Small Catechism*, in the directions for Morning and Evening Prayer, we are told, "In the morning, when you get up . . . ." or, "In the evening, when you go to bed, make the sign of the holy cross and say: In the name of the Father and of the Son and of the Holy Ghost. Amen." Actually Luther worded it more strongly: "Sollt Du Dich segenen mit dem heiligen Kreuz." "You **shall** bless yourself with the holy cross." He did not think of this as an optional activity.

Fortunately, even though the Sign of the Cross was largely ignored for a generation or three in Lutheran circles, it was never completely abandoned. Our old *Lutheran Hymnal* included this rubric in small print in the front of the book: "The sign of the cross may be made at the Trinitarian Invocation and at the words of the Nicene Creed 'and the life of the world to come.' "[2] Granted it was a so-called "permissive" rubric, not a flat-out command, but at least the intention was there. And in our present *Book of Worship* it's hard to miss, printed in red (as rubrics ought to be) right at the beginning of the Brief Order for Confession and Forgiveness: "The sign of the cross may be made by all in remembrance of their Baptism."

So that is when you do it. Right at the beginning of worship, almost as soon as you come into church. For it is a reminder of our baptism. The first time anyone ever made the Sign of the Cross over us was when we were baptized "in the name of the Father and of the Son and of the Holy Spirit." So every time we repeat that sign we are recalling our baptism.

Perhaps you have been in some churches where there are little dishes of so-called holy water near the door of the church. Now you know why they are there. Worshipers can dip their fingers in water and make the Sign of the Cross as they enter the church building, for it was through the sacrament of Holy Baptism that they entered the church, that is, the people of God.

So you can make the Sign of the Cross at the very beginning of your worship, and then again logically at the end when we share the final Blessing. When we teach young children about this ceremony we tell them that the pastor is "tossing the blessing in your direction" so you can "catch it" and paint it on yourself. That's not a bad idea; try it, you'll like it.

And if you like it for starting and stopping your worship, you might find a few other places during the service where it seems to fit. One such place is at the final phrase in the creed, where we confess our belief in the resurrection and eternal life. Another place is during the Sanctus before the Eucharistic Prayer at the phrase "Blessed is he who comes in the name of the Lord." Some people cross themselves right before or after they receive the bread and wine at Holy Communion.

So if you are looking for the customary times for crossing yourself, those are the ones: at the Invocation, at the end of the Creed, during the Sanctus, before or after receiving Communion, and at the final Blessing. But understand there are no hard and fast rules about this thing.

If the Sign of the Cross is not a useful devotion for you, there is little point in just going through the motions. On the other hand, if this is a true reminder of your baptism, then use it as often as you can or care. Use it in your private devotions at home; repeat it as a small act of worship throughout the day.

Indeed, if there is anything that defines who you are as a Christian man or woman, as a Christian boy or girl, it is your baptism. For in that holy washing everything that is unclean about us was washed away. We can understand what the ancient psalmist was driving at when he pleaded with God, "Be thorough at washing me from my iniquity, and from my sins cleanse me." That poignant cry was first sung hundreds of years before Jesus was born.

But our brother Christ was responding to that heart-felt desire when he gave his followers their marching orders. In Matthew's gospel the last thing our risen Lord did before he left was to give us a promise and a task. "I will always be with you," he said; that is his promise. "Disciples all nations," he said; that is his command. "Here's how you will do it," he added. "Do it by baptizing and by teaching." So we are baptized in the name of the Triune God, and we are fashioned into his disciples, and we are thereby given our true identity.

You know how hard it is to have a sense of real identity in a world which tries to turn everyone of us into indistinguishable ciphers. You know how hard it is to muster any sense of self-worth in a society that keeps telling us you have to be Number One or you're nothing. It is sad to see the pathetic things people will do just to gain a little recognition, a dab of attention.

The past two or three years you have noticed a new two-word slogan showing up all over. It started on bumper stickers on the back of rusty pick-ups. Now you can see it on baseball caps and across the front of tee-shirts. "Stuff Happens," it says. Except, of course, the word isn't "stuff;" it's a shorter four-letter word that also begins with S. You could take it as a kind of jaded matter-of-fact statement for people who think they're always getting the short end of the stick. But after a while you realize that people display it because they think that's a cute way of getting attention or making an impact.

What a sad and sorry display: to plaster on the front of your person a slogan that will only make people think you are worth nothing more than a pile of manure, that you are one of the universe's accidental mistakes. But in a world that is so large and that turns us into such anonymous creatures, is it any wonder people are so desperate for any sense of identity, any hint that they may be worth something?

Brothers and Sisters, that is perhaps the finest gift God gives us through our baptism into Christ. We have been washed and named with God's holy Name. Now we belong. Now we are good. Now we are worth while, because we are worth something to God.

When our brother Jesus died on that cross, he did it so that we might each and all know for sure how determined our God is to love and forgive and redeem us. When he rose from the dead that was God's way of assuring us that life is valuable and victorious and that we share in that life now and forever.

When we were baptized, as the apostle says, we were buried and raised with Christ. And all of that, the cross and our baptism, are brought together in one simple devotion, the Sign of the Cross.

You do that in the morning when you get up, and you will know who you are the whole day through. Do that when you crawl into bed, and you will sleep easy. Because under the Sign of the Cross, and in the remembrance of our baptism, is every good thing we need to know about ourselves.

In the Name of the Father, and of the Son, and of the Holy Spirit. Amen.

Confession And The
Bending Of Knees

*Come, let us prostrate ourselves and bow
down,
let us kneel before Yahweh our maker,
for he is our God
and we ourselves are a people of his
pasturing,
sheep of his hand.*

— *Psalm 95:6-7*

*If we confess our sins, trustworthy is he and
just, so that he might remit us our sins and
cleanse us from every injustice.*

— *1 John 1:9*

A basic fact of human life is that no matter what else we
may be, we are surely bodies. We have minds and personalities and souls, to be sure, but these are all connected to our
bodies. Which means we can do nothing without getting our
bodies involved in the process. That is especially true of our
worship. Now I know Jesus once said, "You shall worship
in spirit and truth." But he did not mean to say that truthful,
spiritual worship is something that happens apart from our
bodies. That would be impossible in any case, and a lot less
interesting.

This is why we are spending these nine weeks exploring the
meaning of our *Rituals of Redemption*. For we are convinced
that the best way to get our selves involved in our worship is
by letting our bodies in on the action. Therefore our gestures
and postures and movements, in other words, our ceremonies
and rituals, are crucial for what we do here. For we express
our faith and experience the meaning of our redemption not

only with our voices in word and song but also with our actions. If our words express the content of what we believe, the ritual actions express something of our attitude toward what we believe. For these are our *Rituals of Redemption.*

Perhaps no complex of ceremonies so betrays our attitude as does bending our knees and bodies when we kneel and bow. That is because these postures are so foreign to our everyday motions. We are used to standing. We are used to sitting. And we spend about a third of our lives lying down. These positions seem natural and common. But we don't do much kneeling or bowing, do we?

People used to do it all the time. Especially if the people were "nobodies," and they found themselves in the presence of "somebodies." In other words, when peasants were summoned before the king, they bowed. They knelt down and stretched out flat before the royal throne. Or it was "off with their heads." That kind of groveling was forced upon people, and none of us would appreciate being forced to do that sort of thing today. That sort of nonsense is reserved for freshman initiation rites at university frat houses.

But what if one undertakes to kneel or bow voluntarily? What if we decide to do this as part of our worship? What do our kneeling and bowing reveal about our attitude toward God, about our attitude toward ourselves? Obviously bending our knees and bodies is a sign of respect and a gesture of humility. And maybe there are times when that is simply the most honest posture we can affect.

When the ancient psalmist thought about how Yahweh, the Lord God of his people, had made them and rescued them, how he had shepherded them and kept them safe, he was moved to call his people to their knees. "Come, let us prostrate ourselves and bow down; let us kneel before Yahweh our maker," the poet sang. "For he is our God, and we ourselves are a people of his pasturing, sheep of his hand."

The way we sing this psalm from our hymnals or read it in our Bibles it often says, "O come, let us **worship** and bow down." But that Hebrew word we usually translate as "worship" really means to "kneel" or "prostrate oneself." It's that flat-on-the-ground face-in-the-dust attitude that sweeps over us sometimes when we realize how little importance and significance any single one of us as individuals really has in the grand scheme of the cosmos.

But there is another time, a more significant time, when the humble attitude symbolized by kneeling is most important. That is when we are wrong. When we are honest enough to recognize that we have failed to do what we ought to have done, that we have done something we ought not to have done, that we have wronged others, wronged God, wronged ourselves, that we are in the wrong. . . . That is what can knock us to our knees.

That is the time for a humble confession of sins. Have you noticed the only time in the regular order of worship that our hymnal suggests we kneel is at the confession of sins? The other rubics throughout the service note when we should stand or sit, but halfway through the Brief Order for Confession and Forgiveness is the only time it suggests we kneel. Down on our knees seems to be an especially appropriate posture when we are confessing our sins, doesn't it?

And it's not a bad place to be when we hear the absolving word of forgiveness. There is a line from the Bible which we read to put this entire kneeling, confessing, absolving business in perspective. The apostle says, "If we confess our sins, trustworthy is he and just, so that he might remit us our sins and cleanse us from every injustice." The point is, the forgiveness of our sins is a gift. It is God's gift to us, not something we have earned. And therefore by kneeling when we hear the absolution and receive the gift of forgiveness, our kneeling is also an expression of our receptive attitude. Thus kneeling is appropriate for confessing a sin, and it is just as appropriate for receiving a gift.

Before we ramble on about other times and places where kneeling and bowing are useful, let's explore this more deeply. Kneeling is appropriate for confessing a sin, and it is just as appropriate for receiving a gift. What is at stake here is our basic integrity. We're talking about an honest assessment of who we are and what we are doing with our lives, our integrity as men and women, boys and girls.

A few years ago we were treated to a sorry display of what happens when a person lacks that kind of basic integrity. A jury in South Carolina empaneled for the trial of a so-called televangelist found the man guilty on all charges of using his position to defraud the very folks who trusted him the most. Perhaps you saw his response as a "sound bite" on the 10 o'clock news. "I was innocent when I went in," he said, "and I'm just as innocent now that it's over." The evidence be damned, the jury be hanged, this man refused to admit he was wrong.

Psychologists could tell you, however, that this is just a ploy. Such a protest of innocence in the face of overwhelming guilt is nothing more than a last desperate attempt to avoid facing up to the truth. It's not so much a ruse as it is a sad case of self-denial. It's the very opposite of integrity.

Thank God most of us will never have our lack of integrity displayed in such a public forum, on such a grand scale. For most of us most of the time our sins and failures are more private, more close to home. Maybe only our spouses or children or parents or closest companions will smell us when things go rotten. But even then we need some way of getting things put right again, some honest attitude that will allow our integrity to be restored.

That, of course, is where confession and the bending of knees come in. This is our way of taking an honest look at ourselves, a mechanism for self-evaluation, an attitude which promotes integrity. That's what confession is really all about. But it is more than that. It is also hearing the word of forgiveness and receiving the gift of acceptance. It means learning to affirm all that is good about us precisely because we recognize our goodnesses as gifts from God. And on our knees is the posture for doing that, because kneeling is appropriate for confessing a sin and just as appropriate for receiving a gift.

If so, there may be other times when kneeling or bowing fit what we are doing during worship. When the cross is carried in procession through our midst it is good for us to bow. For here is the reminder of Christ's gift of himself for us, and now we gather around that sign of our worship.

When we receive Christ's body and blood with the bread and wine of Holy Communion, what more natural posture is there than kneeling for this gift? Furthermore, because the high altar is the place where we focus our celebration of this sacrament, it is appropriate to bow in reverence before it.

The ministers bow as they enter or leave the chancel. Worshipers, too, may bow toward the altar, or even genuflect, when they enter their pews. You may feel awkward when you try it — if you try it — for the first time, but at least recognize that this is not a meaningless custom.

And when we say our prayers, especially the petitions of the church on behalf of the entire church, the whole world and our own parish and personal needs, is it not appropriate for us to kneel as we make our requests humbly and anticipate receiving the gift of God's answer? Admittedly in New Testament times the people apparently stood with their hands upraised as they prayed. That, too, could be a meaningful posture for us. But kneeling for prayer is no less meaningful.

And do you remember the line from the canticle from Philippians 2, "At the name of Jesus every knee shall bow?" We can take that as permission at least to bow our heads when the name of Jesus is pronounced during our worhsip. Try doing that and you will surely have to pay attention!

Then for good measure look for the phrases "born of the Virgin Mary" or "he was made man" in the creeds. You may bow then to recognize that the Incarnation is God's gift of himself when the Word became flesh. Or whenever the Gloria Patri is chanted: "Glory be to the Father and to the Son and to the Holy Spirit." Again you may bow in reverence. Or at the beginning of the Sanctus before the Eucharistic Prayer: "Holy, holy, holy, Lord." Just as the prophet Isaiah trembled with woe when he saw the heavenly throne and the six-winged seraphim, so we bow as we realize Christ will be present before us in his holy supper.

That's a lot of kneeling: for confessing our sins and saying our prayers and receiving Communion. And that's a lot of bowing: before the cross and the altar, at the name of Jesus, during the creed, for the Gloria Patri and the Hosanna. But the trick is not remembering when to do it. The trick is to keep it honest.

For kneeling and bowing are expressions of an attitude, an attitude of honest self-evaluation and an attitude of realistic acceptance. The whole point is integrity. Remember when Jesus healed those ten lepers? You know the story from the gospel. Only one of them returned. Surprisingly, it was the one foreigner in the bunch. But he returned to say thank you. More specifically Luke puts it this way. "One of them, seeing he was healed, returned, glorifying God with a loud voice, and he fell on his face at Jesus' feet, thanking him." (Luke 17:15-16)

Flat down on the ground! That's where you acknowledge that you are graced and gifted by God. That's what you do when you say thank you; you bow and you kneel.

Brothers and Sisters, we too have been graced. Our brother Jesus has shared his life with us. He has given us permission to be honest with ourselves and so preserve our integrity. He lived the kind of life he did so that our lives can be genuine. His wholeness and holiness put the lie to our own phoney pretensions.

And his acceptance and forgiveness allow us to enjoy living anyhow. His execution outside Jerusalem was the ultimate gift which exposes our sin and effects our salvation. His restoration to us joyful and victorious is God's affirmation of genuine life.

How we accept that gift says something about our own integrity. Of course, just the motions of kneeling and bowing can be so much fakery. But at least they let our bodies get in on the action; at least they can promote a right attitude, and if a right attitude, then a right heart. Amen.

Preaching And The
Reading Of The Gospel

I preached righteousness in the large assembly.
Look, I did not shut my lips, as you
    yourself know, Yahweh;
Your righteousness I did not hide in the
    middle of my heart.
I told about your truthfulness and your
    deliverance;
I did not hide your mercifulness and your
    truthfulness from the large assembly.
                 — Psalm 40:9-10

For you remember, brothers and sisters, our
labor and toil. Working night and day so as
not to weigh you down, we preached to you
the gospel of God.
                 — 1 Thessalonians 2:9

Everybody loves a parade. Perhaps that is because parades are such extravagantly happy affairs, but also because the sense of motion, of coming and going, resonates inside us in a moving way. You can sit on your blanket in front of the bandstand and listen to the musicians play *Washington Post* and be moved by the experience. But then you can stand at curb side and listen to the same band playing the same tune as they come marching up the street, pass in front of you, and disappear down the block. And that experience will have a little extra pizzazz. It's a parade, you see, and everybody loves a parade.

We don't have parades in church, we have processions. Seldom are our churchly processions as hand-clapping exciting as a circus parade, but they too are moving experiences. They too have the capacity to give parts of our worship a little extra pizzazz. For processions, too, are among our *Rituals of Redemption*, by which we involve our bodies in our worship so we can better experience the ways of our God, whose redeeming love makes us his people.

Which brings us to one of the most important parts of our worship each week. In our Inquirers' Class we take time to review the order of Holy Communion. Then I ask, "Which do you think is the most important part of the service?" Usually someone will answer, "The sermon." Which is quite flattering, of course. But then I have to explain, "No, the sermon may be the longest part of the service, but it is not intended to be the most important part." With any luck at all, someone else will guess the Communion, the distribution and receiving of the bread and wine which are the body and blood of Christ. That person gets a pat on the head.

Then I ask, "And what is the second most important part of the service?" That usually stumps them. They'll try the Lord's Prayer, or a hymn, or the Offering. I hate to discourage that one, but eventually we narrow down the options until someone suggests the Bible readings. So I ask them, "Which one?" And finally they'll get it: the Holy Gospel. The reading of the Gospel is the second most important part of the service.

You see, when we read a portion from one of the New Testament gospels we are not only reading *about* our Lord Jesus, but often as not we are actually *listening to* him. We are hearing what he has to say to us. Just as Christ becomes present for us in the sacramental meal, so his word becomes present for us in the scriptural reading. That is why we surround this reading with special ceremonies. We sit for the other Lessons; we stand for the Gospel. We chant acclamations at its introduction and conclusion: "Glory to you, O Lord." "Praise to you, O Christ." We sing Alleluias as the Gospel book is carried to the place where it will be read.

On major feasts and festivals we will process with the cross and torches down the center aisle and read the Gospel in the midst of the congregation. Those of you in the front pews will turn so that we are all facing the action.

That is the parade we were talking about.

As Christ arrives to speak in our midst through the reading of the Holy Gospel, we make an occasion out of it, standing and processing and chanting. If you think our modest processions are something, you should see how they do it in Eastern Orthodox circles. There the Gospel procession is known as the "minor procession" or the "little entrance"; the book is often covered in gold and jewels, and the parade is quite an impressive ceremony. Which is as it ought to be, if we really believe that our Lord is present when his word is shared.

By the way, you may have noticed that when we pray Matins we normally do include a reading from one of the gospels, but we simply list it as "the Third Lesson"; we don't call it "the Gospel for the Day" in the order of Morning Prayer, and we remain seated. This is because Matins is a more reflective, prayerful service; it is not nearly as celebrative as the Holy Communion liturgy. Morning Prayer is primarily our response to God; the Holy Communion service is primarily God's gift of himself to us.

Well, if the reading of the Gospel is all that important, you might guess that the selections have been carefully chosen. The lectionary in common use by most Christian churches today works on a three-year cycle. One year most of the Gospels are from Matthew; the next year they are from Mark; the third year from Luke. John's gospel fills in all three years, especially during Lent and Eastertide. You can tell we are in the tail end of the third year right now, for today's Gospel is from Luke. Starting in December we will begin reading from Matthew again.

As you become more familiar with the liturgical seasons and cycles, you will recognize that the First Lesson, usually a reading from the Old Testament, is normally chosen to complement the Gospel. So, for example, today's First Lesson from Genesis (32:22-30) is the story of Jacob's wrestling with the angel by the brook Jabbok until he received the blessing he wanted. His persistence serves as an interesting comparison beside Jesus' parable about the so-called importunate widow in today's Gospel; she persisted in appealing to that judge until she got the verdict she wanted. (Luke 18:1-8) The Old Testament reading complements the Gospel.

However, the Second Lesson which is usually from one of the New Testament epistles, runs on an independent track and is normally not calculated to correspond to the Gospel except on important festivals like Christmas and Easter.

The upshot of all this is that the reading of the Holy Gospel, which we celebrate with ritual acclamation and ceremonious procession, not only is a high point of our weekly worship but actually sets the tone for our entire liturgical year.

Now what about the sermon? As a general rule of thumb you can expect that the sermon you hear will be based on the Gospel or one of the other Lessons, or at least on a text which reflects one of the themes of the day's readings. In Lutheran circles so-called "free texts" for preaching are more the exception than the rule. (Obviously this present series of sermons on the *Rituals of Redemption* is an exception to the general rule.)

Basically we expect our sermons to explain the Gospel or Lessons and then to apply them to our daily living. No matter how clever or ordinary, no matter how interesting or boring any sermon may be, you should expect to hear one of the Lessons laid out and explained at some length. And you should expect the preacher to take a stab at applying the Scripture to some issue of importance in our lives as modern men and women.

As you listen for those 10 to 20 minutes, there are two other concerns you may watch for. The first has to do with what we call Law and Gospel. Now don't be confused here. When we talk about reading "the Holy Gospel" in the service, we are talking about a passage from the first four books of the New Testament. When we talk about "Law and Gospel" in this context we do not mean a particular chapter and verse as much as we mean the effect which any biblical passage has on us. We are talking about how the Scriptures impact us.

When God speaks to us, either we will feel bad, or we will feel good at what we hear. Whenever we get the message that we have done wrong and therefore are in the wrong as far as God is concerned, that is God's Law at work. And whenever we learn that we are loved and forgiven by God in spite of ourselves that is the Gospel at work. Law and Gospel are God's twin actions of damning and forgiving, of condemning and saving, of putting us down and lifting us up.

When we were youngsters in Catechumens Class they used to teach us that the letters S.O.S. summarize both Law and Gospel. The Law "Shows us Our Sins," and the Gospel "Shows us Our Savior." How true. Law is thumbs down, Gospel is thumbs up.

The word of the Law is discouraging; the Gospel is eminently encouraging. However you slice it, every word from God has the impact of either Law or Gospel, and you can expect to hear that impact and feel that tension in every sermon.

But more importantly you can expect that the last word, the definitive word, will be a word of Gospel. The Law never helps us out, it only helps us recognize the predicament we are in as human beings. It is the Gospel which frees and forgives us and enables us to get on with living as joy-filled responsible men and women.

It is too bad that we tend to think of the Old Testament as being mostly Law. Which is why the psalm chosen as one of our texts emphasizes just the opposite. Here the psalmist brags about the good things that he has been preaching in the congregation of the people. He has been announcing God's righteousness and truthfulness, his salvation and mercifulness. In other words, the poet sings because he has been sharing Gospel.

I preached righteousness in the large assembly.
Look, I did not shut my lips, as you yourself know,
*   Yahweh;*
Your righteousness I did not hide in the middle of my
*   heart.*

25

I told you about your truthfulnes and your deliverance;
I did not hide your mercifulness and your truthfulness
from the large assembly.

To repeat, the last word is Good News; it is Gospel. Which brings us to the second thing you can expect to find in every sermon. You can expect that this Good News will be grounded in our brother Jesus. That man was so incredibly adept at being able to say or do just the right thing to encourage or inspire people when they were feeling their worst.

Dumb fishermen, lepers, Peter's mother-in-law with her fever and headache, a woman of the streets, a desperate army captain, renegade tax collectors, an all but dead criminal. What a knack Jesus had for covering what was worst about them and for calling forth what was best within them. He was — he is — Gospel personified. And something of that Good News must be shared in every good sermon.

When the apostle Paul was trekking along the Via Egnatia around the shores of the Aegean Sea, he stopped at the free city of Thessalonica long enough to preach and establish a Christian congregation. Some months later when he wrote back to his old friends in order to straighten out a few problems, he reminded them of how he had behaved when he was with them.

"You remember, brothers, our labors and toil," he said. "Working night and day so as not to weigh you down, we preached to you the gospel of God." God's gospel, you see, is not the sort of thing that "weighs you down." It lifts you up, it encourages you; it does not weigh you down.

In the apostle's day traveling preachers were a dime a dozen. They would blow into town, preach a good line, invite themselves into your home, and take up a collection. Before they were through their "Good News" might cost you a pretty penny. You could be paying for their expenses on your MasterCard for months to come. Paul's visit was not like that, he reminded his friends, and so encouraged them to get back to their jobs and cabbage patches and quit sponging off the church. When he was there he worked sixteen hours a day to support himself so he would not be a burden to his new converts. God's gospel will not become a burden to anyone; it is truly Good News, and that is because it is news of our man Jesus.

Brothers and Sisters, we live in a world that is dying for some of that good news. You read the headlines. Taxes go up; the stock market takes a dive; another drunk driver kills a pregnant mother and two of her youngsters; mortar rounds break the cease-fire in Lebanon and another 30 civilians die; another crack house is raided. We have more bad news than we can stomach, coming at us from six directions at once. We're so starved for some good news that a trade for an over-paid football player takes over the entire front page! That got as much space as the end of World War Two.

But it's not just the news *around* us, it's the news *about* us that weighs us down. And we don't need newspaper headlines to tell us what we already know about ourselves. Those little moments of truth we try to ignore tell us all we need to know, and they confirm our worst suspicions. They remind us of how lazy we are, how uncaring and suspicious we can be, how we say some of the nastiest things to the people we think we love the most. It seems as though no matter how much we do right, something in the back of our heads tells us that's not enough and we have to do more.

Then perversely our built-in insecurities start acting up and before we know it we end up putting somebody else down in the desperate hope we will look good in comparison. What a deep and thoroughgoing nastiness there lies within us! Now can we speak Gospel to ourselves and to others? Can we realize the incredibly good news that all of that has been covered by God, for Christ's sake? Can we share something of that liberating word with our spouses and children, with our parents and friends, with our schoolmates and roommates and coworkers?

Boy, if we can make that happen whether by our attitudes and actions or even in so many words, I think people would stand up and cheer! That would be better than a parade! Amen.

Music And The
Singing Of Hymns

Ring out, you righteous, with Yahweh,
  praise suits upstanding people.
Applaud Yahweh with a lyre,
  with a lute make a tune for him,
sing to him a new song,
  do good at plucking string with shouts!
                                    — *Psalm 33:1-3*

Let the word of Christ live in you richly,
as you teach with all wisdom and inspire one
another, as you sing psalms, hymns, spiritual
odes with joy in your hearts to God.
                                    — *Colossians 3:16*

All month we have been talking about our *Rituals of Redemption*, the ceremonies and traditions we follow as we worship the God and Father of our Lord Jesus Christ in this place. The way we cross ourselves, when we kneel and bow, how we process at the reading of the Gospel — all are ways we get our bodies into our worship. And if our bodies are involved, then we are involved.

Yet it is not just the esoteric movements and gestures we need to examine; we will do well also to consider one of the most common ways we have of participating in worship. We need to think about what is happening when we sing and make music. We Lutherans are so good at singing that we can almost assume uncritically that such music is unquestionably part and parcel of worship.

In some senses it is, of course. One of the most recent volumes to roll off the Augsburg-Fortress presses is a collection of devotional reflections for parish musicians. It is titled,

How Can I Keep From Singing? Indeed, how can we keep from singing? It seems so natural, so necessary.

An article on *Music as Worship* in one of my reference works begins by noting that "for most primitive peoples the origin of life is a sound; it was God's hum, shout, croak, or gibber that stirred creation within the void." Furthermore, life begins for each of us with a birthing cry. So "no wonder music and the numinous have always been inseparable."³ In other words, it is almost a primitive impulse that compels us to sing and make music when we worship.

Maybe that is why we can identify with the psalmist as he calls his people to bang on their guitars and strum their harps and pluck their lutes and sing fresh songs. Today's text is the opening stanza of one of Israel's great liturgical paeans. Here the lead singer calls on the entire congregation to join in praise to their Lord and God, to open their throats and make the kind of music that will rock the posts and challenge the sky.

> *Ring out, you righteous, with Yahweh,*
> *praise suits upstanding people.*
> *Applaud Yahweh with a lyre,*
> *with a lute make a tune for him,*
> *sing to him a new song,*
> *do good at plucking strings with shouts!*

You can imagine the swaying crowds packing the temple courts as they pickup the chant, clap their hands, and start to sing.

We don't do a bad job ourselves, do we? Many of you must have been here two summers ago on the special Sunday when we invited the cantor from the Temple Israel synagogue to address our adult forum. His task was to share with us some insights into Jewish worship. He also participated in our service by singing the psalm and a traditional Jewish invitation to hear the Scriptures read.

That morning our own cantor decided to show off what we could do. So he selected a song based on an Old Testament

text as the Hymn of the Day, "The God of Abraham Praise."[4]
It is not an easy one, nor a short one. It goes on for eleven
stanzas! We sang it together in unison, we sang it in harmo-
ny. The women sang alone, the men sang alone. The organ
played a stanza while we kept silence. We even sang it in can-
on without the benefit of prior practice. The women began
a stanza and the men started up two measures later; then the
men began and the women followed. I cannot recall another
time I have had so much fun singing a hymn, and the rest of
you were obviously enjoying yourselves also. We pulled it off
without a hitch.

We are good at singing. We have a reputation throughout
the Twin Cities for being a congregation that knows how to
sing well. Even if you are confronted with a hymn you've never
sung before, that does not have a familiar melody, you manage
to rise to the challenge. And by the third stanza it seems as
though all have learned it and are singing with gusto.

In the little advertising pamphlets our evangelism callers
share with visitors we list some of our parish's selling points.
Among them we claim "an extensive program for music and
the fine arts" and "a tradition of excellent music and singing." And that's the truth. But let's be careful, before we get
so swell-headed and self-congratulatory that we sound uncom-
fortably like the Pharisee in Jesus' story and go down to our
houses unjustified. Let's back off a few paces and take a clearer
look at what we are doing when we sing and make music. Let's
be sure we understand what's happening.

The minister's edition of our *Book of Worship* contains
a directive that sums it up well:

> *Wherever music is employed in the service, and by
> whatever instruments or voices, it should be high-quality
> examples of the art of composition, not cloud commu-
> nication of the content and mood of the service with mu-
> sical triteness or associations bordering on sentimentality,
> and be within the ability of the performers at hand to
> play or sing with assurance.*[5]

31

You notice two things about that rubric. First, it insists that whatever we do, we do it a well as we can. Church is no place for sloppy music or half-hearted singing. The reason for that is because our music and singing of hymns are part of our offering to God. And when we are offering ourselves to God, nothing less than our best is acceptable. Our congregation is so richly blessed with musical ability that we can expect an unusually high level of technical production here. Other parishes do not enjoy the luxuries of a professional cantor or an extraordinary pipe organ or a panoply of skilled musicians. But of course such factors have no bearing on the essential worth and meaning of our worship. What counts is how well we use the gifts with which we have been blessed.

And, second, no saccharine sentimentality, please. Because in musical terms sentimentality focuses our thoughts and feelings inward upon our selves. But the offering of our music and hymns is not intended to glorify ourselves, but to be an act of worship and praise focused on the God who creates and redeems and sanctifies us. To be sure, deciding what is "objective" and therefore more desirable *versus* what is "subjective" and therefore less desirable is not an exact science. Choosing hymns and music involves more than a modicum of what we call "good taste" and "personal opinion." Yet that is our intention, to play the kind of music and sing the kind of hymns which will enable us to direct our selves outward in praise to God.

That is why we stand up to sing most of our hymns, not just because we sing better when we are standing, but because that puts us in a posture of praise. Even when we are seated and come to one of those closing stanzas of praise to the Triune God we expect to hear the bells on the zimbelstern reminding us to stand for the doxology.

When I asked our cantor if there was anything about hymns that he would like me to share in this sermon, he thought a moment and then said, "Tell them to sing sensitively. Tell them to pay attention to the accompaniment and see how the music affects the words."

32

Underlying this entire concern is the fact that all of our hymns and most of our other music are based on biblical texts. The music is the bearer of the word, enlarging and enriching it. The Bible doesn't give us very much in the line of specific directions for our worship, much less for our music, but there is at least one passage which clarifies the relationship between word and music. It is the other text for today.

Let the word of Christ live in you richly, as you teach with all wisdom and inspire one another, as you sing psalms, hymns, spiritual odes with joy in your hearts to God.

See how the apostle stacks up our priorities. First in importance is the word of Christ in our lives, that word of Law which critiques our behavior and judges us for the sinners we are, plus that word of Gospel which uplifts and encourages us with the assurance of Christ's love and forgiveness. That is the word we teach; there is the source of our inspiration and admonition. But running a close second is the music of our worship, our psalms and hymns and spiritual songs which express the joy bursting from our hearts.

That's the beauty of it all, the sheer fact that there is beauty in the way we worship. When the Spirit of God wafted over the primal depths and called forth the orb of this earth, the Lord God looked at all of creation and said, "That is good." But it does not always look as good today, does it? There is so much shabbiness in our urban landscape that sometimes you have to hunt for beauty. There is so much eroding our rural landscape that sometimes we wonder whether we will be able to preserve anything lovely.

But the problem is hardly new. Don't you think they suffered under drabness and shabbiness in Jesus' day too? But our brother had a way of spotting the beauty and calling for joy. "The lilies of the valley," he reminded us, "are more beautiful than Solomon's vestments." (Matthew 6:28-29) "I have come for the joy of it," he said, "that you may have joy." (John 15:11)

Can there be anything uglier than the sight of that man strung up outside Jerusalem, exposed, gawked at, taunted, matted with blood, athirst and deserted? Watch him die, and you will wonder where goodness has fled. But out of that our God has drawn exquisite beauty, extravagant joy, and sheer delight. For he brought our Christ back again, alive and free and full of glory.

Brothers and sisters, do you realize how privileged we are to be able to participate in God's redeeming work in our world? We do so by creating a little beauty around us, too.

The story of Wolfgang Amadaeus Mozart is so well known by now that it seems almost trite to rehearse it. But we remember there were times in his career when he was so shabby and poor that he could not afford kindling to warm his room. He sat with his hands wrapped in woolen socks to keep his fingers warm enough to set notes on paper. But the beauty was there, called forth out of ugliness, and inspiring us today. The constant and gnawing hunger and the incessant chill finally did him in. They called it "consumption" in those days, and he was dead at age 35. Just six people followed his cheap pine coffin, and even they turned back when it started to rain. His pitiful funeral cost exactly $3.10. But out of all that came some of the most beautiful music our ears can hear.

We may not be Mozarts, but our happy task is the same. We confront a world blotted by too much ugliness and shabbiness. And then we sing. Then we make music. And as we do we create the beauty that puts the lie to drabness.

We don't often get fan mail here at the church, but last year about this time someone who lives here in our Powderhorn Park neighborhood sent us this note after he had visited our worship one Sunday:

Dear Rev. Wegener: Yes, I do intend going to your church occasionally. I'm not a Lutheran or even a Christian in a doctrinaire sense but I do feel a touch of the spiritual in your jewel of a church.

It's such a pleasant contrast to the rest of the Chicago-Lake community. Not that I don't like the neighborhood — it's interesting and full of life — but going into your church is a beautiful change of pace. Thanks.

It may not seem like a lot, but you know every time we lift up our voices in another hymn, every time our organ plays another postlude, every time our choirs sing another anthem, every time our musicians play another instrument we are adding to the sum total of beauty in this world. And by God that is good! Amen.

Prayer And The
Burning Of Incense

*Let my prayers be established as smoking
incense before you,
my uplifted hands as an evening grain offering.*
— Psalm 141:2

*And another angel came and stood before
the altar holding a gold censer, and much incense was given to him that he might give it with
the prayers of all the saints upon the golden
altar, the one before the throne, and the smoke
of the incense went up with the prayers of the
saints from the hand of the angel before God.*
— Revelation 8:3-4

We could sit in an austere room to read the Scriptures,
preach a sermon, sing our hymns, speak our prayers, baptize
our children and share our Lord's Supper. And that would
be all right. For what counts is not the fanciness of our service, but the sincere intent of our hearts, and more importantly
the saving Word of God who has redeemed us and made us
his special people for Christ's sake.

But we don't. We have chosen to do our worshiping within
a beautiful sanctuary, one fairly cluttered with symbols, stained
glass and architectual designs calculated to engage our imagination and turn our thoughts Godward. And we invest our
worship with gestures and motions, standing and sitting, bowing and kneeling. Such ceremonies are our *Rituals of Redemption*, calculated to get every part of our bodies into the action,
into our worship. Thus our eyes and ears, our lips and ton-
gues, our arms and legs are all involved.

But not our noses. At least not very much. Two or three
of us can get close enough to the altar flowers to smell their

fragrance; we may catch a hint of the bouquet of the wine when the Communion chalice is presented to us. But seldom do our noses help us worship. Except for a day like today. For today we have fired up the incense pot and you could smell right away that something is different, something is special about today's worship. Which of course is how we have chosen to use this optional accoutrement.

We reserve incense for those feast and festivals which are our high holy days: Christmas and Easter, Reformation and All Saints, Transfiguration and Christ the King, Epiphany and Ascension and Pentecost. In Eastern Orthodox communities incense is a staple. They would scarcely think of celebrating the Divine Liturgy without burning incense. But for us it is an added attraction reserved for special moments.

What makes it special is the simple fact that of all the gestures and rituals we use in our worship, burning incense is the only one which the Bible mentions as a worship ceremony. The Sign of the Cross, kneeling, folding our hands — none of these are even mentioned in the Bible as a worship ceremony. But incense is there, and lots of it.

In Old Testament times during the daily ritual at the temple in Jerusalem the two standard sacrifices were the offerings of two lambs, one in the morning and another again in the evening. While the animal was being burnt on the altar in the main courtyard, the high priest would go inside the Holy Place and burn incense on a smaller altar. Also, while the lamb was offered, "side dishes" of breads and cakes and other cereals would also be offered. So the offerings of meats and breads and incense were part and parcel of the ancient Israelites' regular worship.

You can understand, then, why the psalmist hoped that his prayers would be as pleasing to God as incense and cereal offerings. He was convinced that the Lord God enjoyed the aroma of smoking incense and baking bread, and he trusted that his own prayers would prove equally pleasing. So the psalm we have prayed together catches that hope:

Let my prayers be established as smoking incense before you,
my uplifted hands as an evening grain offering.

With that kind of God-pleasing precedent, it is hard to fault the church for reviving the use of incense just a few centuries after Jesus' day. After all, the Gospels tell us that the angel announced the birth of John the Baptist to Zechariah while he was making that incense offering in the temple one day. And the magi who followed the star to worship the child Jesus included incense in their birthday gifts.

There was a time, to be sure, when Christians avoided incense. For in the earliest centuries of our era offering a pinch of incense on an altar dedicated to the emperor was the key way people could prove that they were not Christians. But by the fourth century, when Emperor Constantine had turned the Christian faith into the official religion of the Roman Empire, our churches were free to use it again.

As you could guess, the traditional patterns have changed over the centuries, but now the general custom is that when incense is used it is especially appropriate at four points in the service: when the ministers enter and leave the church, when we carry the Gospel in procession and read it in the midst of the people, when we present our Offerings at the altar, and when we bless the bread and wine during the Eucharistic Prayer.

You might expect that on Reformation Sunday I would check to see whether Martin Luther had offered any opinion on using incense. Actually he barely ever mentioned the subject. I could find only one instance in which he referred to incense in connection with worship. In his *Formula Missae et Communionis* of 1523, "An Order for Mass and Communion for the Church at Wittenberg," he outlined the liturgy he preferred for the congregation in which he was a member. As he ticks off the items in the service he comes to number six, the Gospel lesson, "for which we neither prohibit nor prescribe candles or incense," he says. "Let these things be free."[6]

So in our freedom as Lutherans we have chosen to use incense from time to time in our worship. So what? Does it have any deeper meaning? Can we invest it with some symbolic importance, other than its obvious olfactory function? We are on the right track when we think of incense as honorific, that is, we use incense at points of honor. So when the thurible is swung in the direction of the altar, we are honoring the symbol of Christ's presence in our midst. When the thurible is swung in your direction let that holy smoke remind you that you are honored and blessed by Christ himself, for he counts you as his special people. You may want to bow in reply.

Incense is honorific. But mostly it is a symbol of prayer. In biblical times people lived on a flat earth and naturally thought of heaven and God's dwelling as up there, beyond the vault of the sky. And as smoke rises heavenward, it was natural to think of it as traveling the same direction as did their prayers. Heaven was up; smoke goes up; prayers go up. It was all one and the same. Today we know better. Our earth is a globe; if heaven is up for us, where is it for Australians? And the planets in our solar system and the billions upon billions of galaxies spin in such a mind-boggling universe that no one would dare point their finger on a celestial map and say, "There. That's where heaven is."

But we have to think of God as somewhere. And whether that somewhere is up there, out there, around there, or in there is beside the point. "Up" will do as well as any, and as long as smoke goes up let it remind us of our prayers.

St. John the Divine had no trouble doing that. In the glorious visions of the End Time which fill so much of the last book of the New Testament we get a picture of what things must be like "up" in heaven. All of the martyrs and saints who have entered their eternal rest are revealed together "below" the heavenly altar. An angel stirs their prayers with the incense and together prayer and smoke ascend to God. But the text tells it better:

And another angel came and stood before the altar holding a gold censer, and much incense was given to him

*that he might give it with the prayers of all the saints upon
the golden altar, the one before the throne, and the smoke
of the incense went up with the prayers of the saints from
the hand of the angel before God.*

What a revelation! What a striking picture that links our prayers with the smoke of incense in such a natural way. Of course, we say, smoke and prayers ascending, incense and prayers so sweet smelling. That's the way it must be. Which means that whenever we do fire up our incense, whether you enjoy the aroma or whether your sinuses rebel, let it remind us of our prayers.

Better yet, let it encourage us in our praying. For when we pray we begin to experience our closeness to God. We Lutherans have taken as our guiding motto the truth that we are justified by God's grace, for Christ's sake, through faith. What that traditional jargon means is that what we could never do under our own steam God has done for us.

When our brother Jesus choked out his last cough on that gibbet near Jerusalem he had done it all. And he had done it for us. Thirty-six hours later when our God hauled him out of his crypt alive and free, he gave us life and freedom. By that dying and by that rising Christ has won our acquittal. We have been pronounced innocent; we are justified. And it is all a gift; none of it is our own earning. God in Christ Jesus lures us into trusting his promise, into investing our faith in the relationship he makes with us. We are, as we say, justified by God's grace, for Christ's sake, through faith.

But how do we get the feel of that justifying? How do we experience such faith? We begin to experience our closeness with God when we start to talk to him, when we begin to say our prayers. Surely there are many good reasons for praying, but chief I think is the simple truth that when we say our prayers we feel the closeness of God. And in his presence we look towards our hearts and practice introspection.

That's a hard commodity to find these days. We spend so much of our time in whatever rat race we have joined, that there are precious few moments off when we can just think about ourselves, our lives, our families, our relationships. The push is always to go faster and perform better and acquire more.

If you are a younger person in school, the endless cycle of assignments and quizzes and papers and tests never lets up. The clear message is that the higher your grade point average or the more successful your athletic team, the better you are. If you are employed, you know perfectly well that the higher you are on the corporate ladder and the more generous your income, the better person you are. If you are retired, the game doesn't quit: the more trips you can take and the more clubs you can belong to, the better you are.

Somewhere along the line we need a chance to remember what is real, and the best chance we have is when we pray. For then we can look inward and listen for the voice of God and hear the assurance that we are God's people not because of our accomplishments, but because of Christ.

When we remember the history of the Reformation, we usually think of Martin Luther as the firebrand who started the movement, as the priest-turned-reformer who dared challenge the ecclesiastical establishment, as the debater and preacher and author. We can too easily forget that by profession he was really a professor, a teacher of Old Testament at the University of Wittenberg. Near the end of his life he was engaged in lecturing on the book of Genesis. When he got the story of Joseph, the favorite younger son of Jacob who was sold into slavery by his brothers, he let his imagination wander. He imagined what it must have been like for Joseph, stuck and stymied in the pharaoh's prison, longing for his family and for freedom. Here are Luther's words:

> Thus Joseph sighs, sobs, and desires to be freed and to be in his father's house . . . But God replies: "I am the Lord your God, whom you are invoking, whom you are censing, and to whom you are offering 'a column of smoke.'

*"I smell and take great delight in the burning of that in-
cense; for the incense of your prayer, faith, and hope has
filled not only My nostrils but also all heaven. I will liber-
ate you in such a way that it will be beyond what you
understand."* [7]

Sisters and Brothers, we may have to make a mental jump
to connect the aroma of incense with our life of prayer. But
even Luther caught the connection instinctively: "the incense
of our prayer, faith and hope filling the nostrils of heaven."
What a necessary idea! With so much busy-ness about us that
we never take time for prayer and introspection, that we seldom reflect on our relationship with God, how good it is that
just a little smoke can call us to prayer. Amen.

Fellowship And The
Kiss Of Peace

Mercy and truth will meet;
justice and peace will kiss.
— *Psalm 85:10*

For the rest, brothers and sisters, rejoice,
prepare yourselves, encourage yourselves, think
the same thoughts, practice peace. And the God
of love and peace will be with you. Greet each
other with a saintly kiss; all the saints greet you.
— *2 Corinthians 13:11-13*

With any luck at all once or twice a year someone gives me a pair of tickets to a Gophers or North Stars hockey game. I grab one of my children and away we go. My daughter hopes for a few good fist fights; my boys hope we're in the seat that wins the door prize. Which means that we do stay in our seats watching the action. We are afraid that if we run to the refreshment stand we might miss a big goal. In other words, we may not know a lot about hockey but we sure do enjoy the action. But you know, if I ever figure out what that "blue line" is all about or when a body check is legal and when it's not, I have an idea I'll enjoy the game even more. For when you are better acquainted with the rules and know something about the strategy, you can't help but grow in your appreciation of the contest.

The same is true about going to church. Anyone can stumble into a church without knowing anything about worship and still appreciate to some degree the music and singing, the praying and preaching, and the general pageantry of the service. But you don't have to come back too often before you realize that our worship is chuckfull of unusual movements and gestures, traditions and ceremonies which obviously have special meaning.

These past weeks we have been dealing with these *Rituals of Redemption*. We call them our *Rituals of Redemption* because they get out bodies, and therefore our selves, involved in the redeeming work of God, who counts us all as holy saints for the sake of our savior Jesus the Christ. But you have to know the rules to appreciate what the rituals mean; you have to understand the strategy to really enjoy the game. And maybe the Sharing of the Peace is one of the least understood ceremonies in our worship.

We didn't always do this, you know. Most of us can remember when the Sharing of the Peace came into our liturgy. Oh, in the older *Lutheran Hymnal* there was the *Pax Domini*, that spot right after the Words of Institution and right before the *Agnus Dei* and the Distribution of Holy Communion when the minister would turn from the altar and say to the people, "The people of the Lord be with you always!" The people would reply with a long "A-men." But we wouldn't turn to each other with a hand-clasp or other greeting. Which was too bad, because all those years we missed a unique chance to exchange one of the most solemn and pregnant gestures in our liturgy. The spoken *Pax Domini* was a remnant of the ancient "kiss of peace" but without the gesture!

No doubt the modern romantic and erotic overtones of kissing mean that we will never resurrect that ancient ritual in its original form. But there was a time in New Testament days when Christian people regularly greeted each other during their worship services with a kiss. And it was not a mere greeting, either. That kiss was a way of sharing the blessings of God, the gifts of joy and love and peace which come from Christ. This was a practical, concrete way all the saints could affirm their common fellowship within the church.

That's why we find it mentioned at the close of several of the New Testament epistles. Take Paul's correspondence with the congregation at Corinth, for example. The problems in that parish make a list as long as your arm. We won't go into the embarrassing details this morning. It is enough to know that if any modern congregation had as many difficulties with sexual indiscretions, cliquish bickering, incipient heresies, disruptive worship services, and anti-clergy biases it would probably be drummed out of the synod.

Paul had to try to deal with that mess. He wrote letter after letter and even made a visit or two trying to straighten things out. It is not clear whether he was entirely successful. Nevertheless, the closing paragraphs of his correspondence contain these helpful thoughts:

> *For the rest, brothers and sisters, rejoice, prepare yourselves, encourage yourselves, think the same thoughts, practice peace. And the God of love and peace will be with you. Greet each other with a saintly kiss; all the saints greet you.*

Remember that when Paul wrote to his congregations it was expected that his letters would be read aloud during their weekly gatherings. So nearly the last thing the people heard was his directive that they share a holy kiss. That kiss would be a sign of God's own love and peace. It would be a sign that all the saints, that is all the Christians with Paul and all the believers at Corinth, were united in a single bond of fellowship.

Well before the year A.D. 200 Christian churches had institutionalized the kiss of peace and made it a regular part of their weekly worship. It came right in the middle, after the Service of the Word and the prayers and right before the people brought their offerings to the altar to begin the Service of the Meal. It had become a sign of God's peace. After all, Jesus had said something about "making peace with your brother or sister before you present your gift to the altar."

Throughout the centuries it was shifted closer and closer to the actual moment of Communion, and at the same time it shifted farther and farther away from being a real kiss, or even a real gesture for that matter. But now we have it back as the Sharing of the Peace right in the middle of our services, after the prayers, right before the Offering. So be sure you know what you are doing here.

When we study the order of worship in our Inquirers' Class we try to put each item in one of two categories on the basis of the direction in which the flow goes between God and the people. So for example the reading of the Lessons and the distribution of Communion are obviously God-to-us. The singing of hymns and the praying of prayers are us-to-God. You can tell which is which because most of the time because the pastor gets to speak God's lines.

Where does the Sharing of the Peace fit? God-to-us? Or us-to-God? It looks more like us-to-us, doesn't it? But don't be confused. This is the one time in the service when you speak God's good word of hope and forgiveness to each other. You turn to your neighbor, clasp your hands, look each other in the eye, and you say, "Peace be with you." And your neighbor will return that word of peace to you.

Understand clearly, this is no time for hellos and how-do-you-dos. This is not a time to get acquainted and share mere greetings. This is the time to share the shalom of God, the peace of the Lord, with your fellow worshipers. This is a time to be welcomed and affirmed as a fellow saint within God's family. Your gesture may be a clasping of hands or a hug and embrace or even a real kiss, whatever is meaningful and comfortable. But the gift is God's gift, shared among his people, face to face. So don't be too quick to sit down. The ushers will get to you with the offering plates soon enough. Let the ministers be your cue; our return to the chancel concludes the Sharing of the Peace.

The minister's edition of our *Book of Worship* explains it all this way:

> *The peace which enables people to live in unity and the spirit of mutual forgiveness comes only from Christ whose Word has been proclaimed. Without the intention to live in such unity, participation in the sacramental celebration is a mockery.*

48

The first exchange is between the presiding minister, speaking in Christ's name, and the entire congregation; it is not optional. Following that, the people may exchange the peace with each other.

Personal exchanges of the peace should be as unpatterned as possible, but its meaning and significance should be kept clear: It is not the occasion merely for conviviality. The choice of gesture, whether a handshake or an embrace, should be left to the persons themselves.[8]

Brothers and Sisters, do you see what is at stake here? Today's psalm uses the figure of a kiss to link together God's blessings of kindness and fair play, truthfulness and wholeness. "Mercy and truth will meet," sings the psalmist, "justice and peace will kiss." Similarly, at the time for the holy kiss our mutual Sharing of the Peace of the Lord allows all God's goodnesses to become incarnate in our midst.

I notice that in some churches' bulletins this point in the service is called "the passing of the peace." It's as though the ministers had the peace and then give it to the first person in each pew who gives it to the second person who gives it to the third person and so on. But we're not passing the Olympic torch from hand to hand. Rather, we are each of us faith-filled men and women, boys and girls, people who share Christ's grace with others. Each of us has received the forgiving word, and now each of us shares this with our neighbor.

Can you imagine what God can do through us? There must be someone within this congregation, perhaps sitting only a pew or two away from you, with whom you do not get along, perhaps someone with whom you have had a significant disagreement. Is it not a profound gesture that we are able to set all that aside as we anticipate communing together before Christ's altar?

Every Sunday there are at least a handful of people who come here because there is no other place to go. They are looking for some word of solace, some sign of acceptance, some token of encouragement to help them through the coming

49

week. Is it not an act of God's grace that we have a chance to turn to them, even though we do not know them, and share so personally that peace of Christ which makes the week bearable?

Our congregation includes a healthy percentage of older people who have never married or have divorced or have been widowed, and we have an equally large number of younger adults who are single or who will never marry. Many of us therefore do not live in a typical family setting. Is it not a marvel of God's love that together we can all be a family, a church family, and symbolize it by Sharing the Peace of the Lord brother to brother and sister to sister?

There is an old story about a famous teacher who sat around a blazing fire with a few of his students late at night. Their meandering conversation was broken by periods of silence when they simply gazed at the stars and the moon. After one of those long silences the teacher asked a question. "How can we know when the night has ended and the day has begun?"

One pupil was quick to volunteer. "You know the night is over and the day has begun," he said, "when you can look off in the distance and tell which animal is your dog and which is the sheep. Is that the right answer, Teacher?" "That is a good answer," replied the teacher thoughtfully, "but not the one I would give."

The disciples fell to talking, and a few minutes later a second offered this answer. "You know the night is over and the day has begun," he said, "when light falls on the leaves and you can tell whether it is a palm tree or a fig tree." Again the teacher shook his head. "That was a fine answer," he said gently, "but not the one I would give."

Now the students' conversation turned into a more desperate discussion, until one of them said, "Teacher, answer your own question, for we cannot think of another reply." So the teacher looked intently into their faces. "When you look into the eyes of another person and see a brother or sister you know that it is morning," he said. "For if you cannot see a sister or brother, it will always be night."[9]

I think our brother Jesus would have agreed, don't you? The evening before they thought they got rid of him he was eating supper with his men. Their after dinner conversation was peppered with hints of the coming disaster. But then, partly to dispel the sense of foreboding, he made them a promise. "Peace I leave with you," he said, "my peace I give to you." (John 14:27)

Within hours they had railroaded him out of town and strung him up. "It's all over!" he cried, and he died, and they speared his side. But it wasn't, was it? Because come Sunday evening he was surprising his people again, joining them in closed rooms, showing off his hands and feet. Remember his greeting? "Peace be with you," he said, "peace be with you." (John 20:19, 21, 26)

Fellow saints, you know now how our Lord keeps sharing that peace with us, don't you? He shares his peace through each of us, not least of all when we clasp each other's hands and make it happen. Who knows, you may be the one to help another feel part of the family of Christ, the communion of saints, the kingdom of God that outlasts even death and touches eternity. Amen.

Sacrifice And The Giving Of Money

Let them laud Yahweh for his mercy,
for his wonderfulness to the children of
humans.
Let them sacrifice sacrifices of thanks,
and sing of his deeds with ringing cries.
— Psalm 107:21-22

You are being enriched in every way for every generosity, which will work out through us into thanksgiving to God. For the service of this ministry is not only more than replenishing the deficiencies of the saints, but is also overflowing with many thanksgivings to God. Through this test of service, you are glorifying God by your obedience to the confession of the gospel of Christ, and by your generosity in the collection for them and for all. And in their petitions for you they are longing for you because of the exceptional grace God put upon you. Thanks to God for his indescribable gift!
— 2 Corinthians 9:11-15

Last month and this we have been using our sermons as times to think about our *Rituals of Redemption*. These are the movements and gestures and traditional ceremonies which accompany our worship. They help us get our bodies, our selves, into the experience of the redeeming love of God, who makes us his special people for the sake of Christ. In a sense we learn to experience and appreciate our redemption through these *Rituals of Redemption*.

53

Some of them seem easier and more natural than others. Singing the hymns and reading the Gospel, for example, are such natural activities we would be hard pressed to worship without them. Other ceremonies, such as making the Sign of the Cross or kneeling and bowing or burning incense, may not be as familiar for many of us and so seem more difficult.

Today we will deal with what may be the most difficult ritual of all. It is difficult not because it is hard to do, not because it is an unfamiliar action. It is difficult because it requires that we sacrifice something of ourselves. It is the collection of the offerings. It is that point in the service when we must reach into our wallets and purses, extract our money, and turn loose of it. Then who knows where it goes?

Did I ever tell you the story about the two Scotsmen who were walking home after church? Suddenly one of them stopped. "Ach, I've done a terrible thing," he said. He pulled two coins from his pocket and stared at them. "I put my gold piece in the offering plate by mistake."

"Well," said his companion, "why not go back to the kirk and explain to the parson what happened; he'll give it back to you." "That's a good idea," said the other, and they started walking back toward the church. But they had only gone a short way when he stopped again. "Nay," he said to his friend, "I'm not going back. I gave that gold to the Lord, and to hell with it!"

Sometimes it is no less easy for us to part with our offerings, which is what makes this such a difficult ritual. So it is good for us to go back to square one and get our thinking straight on this matter. And the most important thing to remember is that our offerings are part of our worship. We could hold the collection basket at the door and you could deposit your donations on your way in or out.

We could send you a bill and you could pay by mail. We could even set up an electronic fund transfer whereby money from your checking account would automatically be moved to the church's account every month. We could do it with your VISA card. But we don't. We take time out of the middle of the service to receive our offerings and present them at the altar and dedicate them to the work of God in this place. In other words, our offerings are part of our worship; they are an act of worship.

Many people don't realize it, but one of the most important things St. Paul ever did was to take up a collection. As he traveled on his journeys throughout Asia Minor and Greece he encouraged all his converts to contribute to a fund he was gathering, a fund he intended to take back to the mother church in Jerusalem to help the Christians there through some tough times. You can tell this was important for Paul, for he mentions this pet project half a dozen times in his letters. It was not easy for him to do. On the one hand it was hard to get some of his churches to cough up the funds; on the other hand he was not sure whether the Jerusalem church would accept his gift. Frankly we don't know how well he succeeded.

We do know that the trip he took to Jerusalem to present the collection was his Waterloo; it was the very time he was arrested and sent on his journey as a prisoner to Rome where he was martyred. Which goes to show that you can really get into hot water if you try to run a special fund appeal! But listen to how the apostle talks about this collection. He doesn't treat it merely as an act of charity. He doesn't appeal merely to his people's sense of generosity. Rather, he loads it with worship language because for him the collection was an act of worship.

> *You are being enriched in every way for every generosity, which will work out through us into thanksgiving to God. For the service of this ministry is not only more than replenishing the deficiencies of the saints, but is also overflowing with many thanksgiving to God.*

> *Through this test of service, you are glorifying God by your obedience to the confession of the gospel of Christ, and by your generosity in the collection for them and for all. And in their petitions for you they are longing for you because of the exceptional grace God put upon you. Thanks to God for his indescribable gift!*

This is a pretty literal translation of this passage in the Greek New Testament, but even so you can't catch all the subtle overtones here. For example, the word "service" is really *diakonia*, a "diaconate," the work of a deacon. The word "ministry" is really "liturgy." "Thanksgiving" is "eucharist." The word for "collection" is *koinonia*, which otherwise means "fellowship." In other words because the Corinthians are such generous "deacons," their worshipful "liturgy" or offering results in many "eucharists" or thanksgivings to God; their collection is really a "fellowship" or partnership in the work of God, a veritable expression of God's grace.

All these words — deacon, liturgy, eucharist, koinonia — are terms for worship; in other words, the collection is an act of worship. So the bottom line for us is the same: Whatever else is going on when the ushers pass the offering plates down our pew, this is not a recess or intermission in the service; rather, it is an act of worship, just as important in its own way as any prayer or hymn.

Even the place in the service where we receive our offerings is important. It begins the second half of the service. The first half, the Service of the Word where we speak to God in our prayers and God to us in the Scriptures, concludes with the Sharing of the Peace. The second half, the Service of the Meal, begins with the Offering. First we offer our gifts to God, and then God offers himself to us in the gift of the Holy Communion. Thus our offering of ourselves, symbolized by our gifts of money, begins the liturgical action which culminates in our Lord's Supper.

Already by A.D. 100 Christians had made the offering a part of their worship. At that point in their services they would bring their gifts of bread and wine and other foods and money to their altars. The priests would take as much of the bread and wine as they would need for their Communion meal, and the rest would be set aside to be distributed later to those in need.

What was symbolized there was the truth that God takes our ordinary stuff, our bread and wine and money, and puts it to extraordinary use. Our ordinary food and drink are returned to us as the sacramental meal which assures us that we are a forgiven people, loved and accepted as the men and boys and women and girls who are God's special people.

Today we try to recapture that truth when we invite members of the congregation to bring the bread and wine to the altar at the same time the gifts of money are presented. Some congregations do this regularly every Sunday; others, like ours, may only do it on special occasions. At other times we place the bread and wine on the altar while the monetary gifts are being gathered. But in any case the two go together: the elements for the Communion and the Offerings of money are our sacrificial offerings. symbols of our determination to give our very selves into God's services in gratitude for all the blessings we enjoy from God.

One of my books on liturgical ceremonies puts it this way:

> *One of the functions of the royal priesthood is to offer sacrifices. These consist of sacrifices of self, prayer, praise, and thanksgiving. We express this offering also in the material gifts of money, in which are included the bread and wine used in the Sacrament of the Altar.*

> *That is why the bread and wine are brought to the altar when the money is collected. The money, bread and wine placed on the altar are a token. A token is something which stands for something else.*

> *The Eucharistic token of material things — money, bread and wine — stands for ourselves. By them and in them we are carried to and placed on the altar of God. They are not merely a donation, but a token of ourselves.*

> *This identification of ourselves with the Eucharistic token is not done automatically. It requires a sacrificial act of the will, of self-giving in response to the grace of God.*

> *When the money, bread, and wine are placed on the altar, we say in effect: "In these material things, O Lord, I offer Thee myself, wholly, unconditionally, with all that*

I am and have." These offerings are not an indifferent
part of the Holy Communion Service; they belong to it
as much as any other part.[10]

Maybe you caught the word "sacrifice" in those paragraphs. We Lutherans have been wary of using the word "sacrifice" to describe our Communion services. We don't want to give the impression that we are in any way earning or meriting God's grace by bringing our offerings or by celebrating this sacrament. But there is another sense in which the word "sacrifice" is just the right term to describe what we are doing, because a scarifice can also be an act of thanksgiving, a way of showing our gratitude for all that God has done for us.

The Old Testament psalmist would have known what we are talking about. In the psalm we chanted earlier the poet sings about all of the times the Lord rescued his people, how he redeemed them and gathered them, fed them and clothed them, brought them to a good land and prospered them. Smack in the middle of this list of God's goodnesses he tells them what they must do: They must offer a sacrifice of thanksgiving.

> *Let them laud Yahweh for his mercy,*
> *for his wonderfulness to the children of humans.*
> *Let them sacrifice sacrifices of thanks,*
> *and sing of his deeds with ringing cries.*

We can identify with that, because that is what we are doing when we pass the plate and pour the wine and break the bread. We are offering our sacrifice of thanksgiving as part of our worship.

And we can dare to make it a genuine offering, a real sacrifice, not merely a contribution or a donation. We can dare to give so generously that we will give up something of ourselves, not merely our leftovers. We can dare to give apples, not apple cores. And we can dare to make that sacrifice because we thank our Christ for the sacrifice he made for us.

He didn't hold much back, you know. He sacrificed his life, his dignity, for us. He was hung up on Calvary's cross, his life offered for us. And our God gave him back to us, lively and generous, so that we might be truly alive and gracious also.

Now in response to our Christ's sacrifice of himself, can we be any less generous in our sacrificial offerings of thanks? Well, you will have to answer that for yourself. But I tell you this, there is an added benefit. For when we give sacrificially we are committing ourselves to a worthy purpose outside of ourselves.

So much of our life is spent just looking out for our own survival and well being. But then that's reality, isn't it? That's just the way things are in this world. But that's no way to enjoy living. Real joy comes when we are able to move beyond ourselves and bring something to other people.

Last Thursday the First Friday Seniors Fellowship attended a production of "The Immigrant" over in St. Paul at the Great North American History Theatre. We were all touched by the story of a Jewish immigrant to Hamilton County, Texas: how he started out peddling bananas from a pushcart and ended up owning a dry goods store on the town square. He was helped by the town banker who gave him the loans he needed when he was getting started.

But there was one revealing scene near the end of the play that caught my eye. The two men, the banker and the former immigrant, got in an argument over a Sabbath supper. And finally the Jewish host said, "I want to give something back. I can't be happy just taking; I have to give something back."

Brothers and Sisters, the same is true for us. There is no joy in just receiving. We have to give something back. That's what makes life worth living, the chance to be committed to some worthy purpose outside of ourselves. It's daring to sacrifice out of a sense of thanksgiving. And we get the chance to do that every time the plate is passed, every time the wine is poured, every time the bread is broken.

You try that for a while, and see what sacrifice and the giving of money will do for you. You will find great joy in offering ordinary stuff for some extraordinary purpose. And you will discover that our brother Jesus can use ordinary people for his extraordinary service. Amen.

Communion And The
Sharing Of The Chalice

*I will raise the cup of deliverance
and call on the name of Yahweh.*
— *Psalm 116:13*

*The cup of the blessing which we bless, is
it not a fellowship in the blood of the Christ?
The loaf which we break, is it not a fellowship
in the body of the Christ? Since a loaf is one,
the many of us are one body. For all of us partake of the one loaf [and the one cup].*
— *1 Corinthians 10:16-17*

If I read "Miss Manner's" column correctly what counts
when you sit down to dinner is not just what you are eating
and drinking but also how you handle your fork and glass.
Not just menu, but manners; not just the substance, but how
you manipulate it. In all of life we have our little rituals and
ceremonies which make a difference because we choose to invest them with meaning and significance.

So if our youngsters stab a pork chop with a fork, pick
up the whole piece of meat and start chewing away, we make
them put it back on their plates and use their knives to cut
off dainty little pieces. Grabbing and chawing the chop may
be all right at a backyard barbecue, but not when you're dining with good china on a tablecloth. Not just the menu, the
manners count too. And here the manners signify considera-
tion and politeness and good breeding.

You wouldn't think that we would need to discuss the etiquette involved with our main meal, our Lord's Supper, but
we do. In fact, over the centuries the protocol surrounding
this sacramental meal has been the focus of no little discussion,

quite a bit of controversy, and from time to time even bloodshed. Who can host it? Who is welcome to dine? What kind of bread, leavened or un? What kind of wine, really fermented or mere juice? (In other words, what is the menu?) Should we stand, sit or kneel? How often should we serve it? And, of course, with what sort of utensils?

That's the one that seems to warrant the most discussion lately. Leave it to the theologians to argue over transubstantiation *versus* sacramental union, or real presence *versus* symbolic presence. Most of us are content to affirm that with this bread and wine we receive Christ's body and blood, and leave it go at that. But how are we going to serve it? That's the question. Specifically, how are we going to drink that wine?

The most ancient way is the most obvious. Jesus raised a single cup, spoke a blessing, and shared it with his people. And they all drank from it. It's as simple as that. So for centuries the church has been following that precedent and offering the communion wine in a common chalice from which all may drink. Except, of course, it is not quite that simple. There was a time in the early Middle Ages when the custom in many places was to have two chalices, a smaller cup for the celebrant and a larger bowl with a pair of handles for the people. And the people would not drink from the bowl directly but sip their wine through a straw or tube.

Then, of course, after about the 12th century, the people didn't get any wine at all; for the western Latin church adopted the custom of withholding the wine from the people, who only received the bread. Except for the Hussites' short-lived attempt, the cup wasn't really restored to the people until the time of the Lutheran Reformers. "Among us both kinds are given to laymen in the sacrament," they insisted. "Concerning the chalice Christ . . . commands with clear words that all should drink of it."[11] You would think that would settle the matter for Lutherans, but it hasn't.

Meanwhile Christians in the Eastern Orthodox churches have become accustomed to receiving the Holy Communion through a form of intinction. There the priest dips the bread in the wine and gives the sacrament to the people, often with a spoon. And in many Protestant congregations the wine is reguarly administered in individual glasses (hopefully real glasses, not disposable paper or plastic items). That pretty well sums up the options: the common chalice, intinction, and individual glasses, whether pre-filled or filled at the altar rail from a chalice with a pouring lip.

You know how we do it in this parish. We have had a long tradition of celebrating the Eucharist using a common chalice; a year and a half ago we added the option of intinction.

Now before we talk about what is really important, namely, the meaning of this particular *Ritual of Redemption*, let's get two other matters out of the way. The first is a review of the sheer mechanics of communing; the second is the minimum-*versus*-maximum principle.

First, the mechanics. When you come to receive the bread which is Christ's body simply hold out your hands, palms up, one resting on another. Then I can place the host in your palm. This is preferable to reaching out with your fingers, which increases the chances that we may embarrass ourselves by dropping the wafer. When the host is in your palm, simply take it with your fingers and put it into your mouth.

Then when the chalice is offered you can help the assisting minister by grabbing the foot of the chalice and helping tip it yourself as you drink a swallow of the wine which is Christ's blood. If you choose to receive the wine by intinction, let the wafer lie in the palm of your hand until the minister comes close to you. Then take it in your fingers and dip it in the smaller cup offered by the acolyte. Neither process is overly complicated; both enable us to share our Lord's Supper in a quietly dignified manner. The mechanics are really not the issue.

Second, a matter of more importance. It has to do with our attitude about this sacrament. When we were first discussing the possibility of adding intinction, one of the comments we heard often went to this effect: "It doesn't make any difference, really, how we receive the wine. Ultimately the only thing that matters is that we receive Christ's blood."

In one sense that is true of course; no matter how we receive the wine we do receive Christ's blood for the forgiveness of our sins and the strengthening of our faith. But in another sense we need to guard against the attitude behind that comment. For the attitude seems to be: "What's the minimum we need to do to receive the benefit?" Don't you think a more positive attitude would ask: "What's the maximum we can do to follow Christ's direction?"

When we get beyond the immediate business of Communion etiquette and start talking about how our faith intersects with our life, we don't want to be asking, "What's the least we can get by with?" Or, "What's the minimum I have to do to qualify as a Christian?" Rather, if we have been touched by the love of God in Christ Jesus how can we help but keep ferreting out more and more ways to show anyone who cares to look that we have found the center of our lives in our brother Jesus?

Our question must be, "What more can I do to let my faith shine through my life?" Or, "What is the maximum impact Christ will have on my actions today?" That concern for the maximum, our maximum commitment to Christ Jesus, is what being a Christian is all about. And it also colors the way we have chosen to share his Supper in our congregation.

Some of you may recall the way we argued the case when we adopted our present parish policy. Here's what we said:

> *Mount Olive Congregation has always cherished the use of the common chalice as the preferred way of distributing the communion wine. This method most closely reflects Jesus' own use and most clearly responds to his command that all should drink of the cup in remembrance of him.*

> *Some communicants, however, are unable to drink the alcohol in the wine. Others, when they have a cold, wish to avoid the appearance of giving germs to others.*

> *Still others find that their concerns for hygiene make it difficult to commune from a chalice; while they respect*

*the sacredness of Christ's presence in the wine which is
his blood, they remain uncomfortable drinking with
others from a common cup.*

I like the attitude behind our policy (and not just because
I wrote the words). The attitude betrays a "maximalist" ap-
proach. It recognizes that we want to do all we can to follow
Jesus' own example. But just as importantly it recognizes that
we want to include all we can in the gift of his sacrament. For
if this sacrament means anything at all, it means that here our
Jesus binds himself to us. And that means we are bound
together with each other. Our Lord's Supper is no solo performance.

It is not like eating the blue plate special on a stool at the
counter in some cafe. It is more like sharing Thanksgiving dinner with your family around the dining room table. And no
paper plate balanced on your knee, thank you. For when we
eat this bread and drink this cup we are united together in communion with each other, in solidarity with each other.

That was the issue, of course, when St. Paul instructed his
congregation at Corinth about these matters. There was a parish bursting at the seams, not because it was growing fast in
numbers, but because the members were splitting into quar-
reling factions and competing cliques. You are making a mock-
ery of our Lord's Supper, warned the apostle. What we have
here is *koinonia*, fellowship, communion.

*The cup of the blessing which we bless, is it not a fellow-
ship in the blood of the Christ? The loaf which we break,
is it not a fellowship in the body of the Christ?*

*Since a loaf is one, the many of us are one body. For
all of us partake of the one loaf [and the one cup].*

You see the logic? The bread and wine are a fellowship
or communion in Christ's body and blood. That's basic; that
underlies everything else. But then there is something else,
something important, something meaningful and symbolical.

It has to do with our unity as a people. We all partake of the one loaf of bread and the one cup of wine, and therefore "the many of us are one body."

Now before you look this passage up in your Bibles and conclude that I am fibbing to you, I want to come clean about this text. The words "and the one cup" are in brackets: "For all of us partake of the one loaf [and the one cup]." The reason is that the best and oldest manuscripts of the Greek New Testament do not include the phrase "and the one cup" at this spot.

Which is rather revealing. It means that somewhere along the line some pious scribe, whether deliberately or not we can only guess, added those words because they seemed so natural and obvious. He sat at his desk one Tuesday afternoon copying the Scriptures by hand. His mind was on automatic pilot. He came to this passage he knew by heart because he heard it so often in the liturgy. Naturally, we are one in Christ because we share the same Communion, the same bread and wine. "For all of us partake of the one loaf and the one cup." And there it was, an added phrase that would tell the truth and bedevil scholars for centuries to come.

That is why the way we choose to share this meal, in other words, our table etiquette, can be called a *Ritual of Redemption*. For even in the way we maximalize our response to Christ both by sharing a common chalice and by broadening our participation via intinction . . . . Either way we are getting our motions, our bodies, our selves, into our worship and thereby acting out the redeeming love God has shown us in our man Jesus. We are embracing our conviction that we who commune together stand in solidarity with each other. And that is no mean blessing.

But we can do better than that; we can go farther than that. Have you noticed that in the first seven sermons in this series when we tried to apply the meaning of our *Rituals of Redemption* to our everyday living, we pretty much zeroed in on personal and congregational benefits.

The Sign of the Cross with its reminder of baptism give us a sense of identity and self-worth. Bending our knees and confessing our sins foster honesty and integrity. Reading the Good News which is the Gospel counters the bad news we hear in so much of life. Making music and singing hymns adds to the sum total of beauty in our world. Incense and praying call us to introspection and reflection. The Sharing of the Peace gives us the feeling of family here. All of these are benefits to ourselves.

Last week we took a tentative step in a broader direction; we suggested that the sacrificial offering of our money gives us a chance to be committed to some worthy purpose outside of ourselves. This week let us go even farther. For by sharing in the Holy Communion we not only put ourselves in solidarity with each other, but we are also put in solidarity with the world.

The ancient psalmist knew something about that. For when he called on the Lord's name and drank his cup of wine he knew it symbolized freedom and liberation, redemption and salvation. "I will raise the cup of deliverance," he sang, "and call on the name of Yahweh!" He knew what the poor and oppressed people of the world know. He knew what those who long for justice and freedom know. And he stood in solidarity with that world.

We too, Brothers and Sisters; we too know how much our friend Jesus cared for the little people in this world. We know how he lived to invite them into his fellowship, how he died as one of them, and how our God raised him for them. Whenever we share the loaf and the cup which are his gift to us, we too, stand in solidarity with him and therefore with them. We stand in solidarity with the world.

About ten years ago an ecumenical, albeit unofficial, group of Christians spent a weekend retreat together in Shakertown, Pennsylvania. They were trying to devise ways they could respond to the world's cries for ecological responsibility and justice. They didn't turn the world upside down. But they made a pact together, and their nine-point "Shakertown Pledge" has inspired an awful lot of people since. Here's what they had to say to each other and to the world:

> *Recognizing that the earth and the fullness thereof is a gift from our gracious God, and that we are called to cherish, nurture, and provide loving stewardship for the earth's resources,*
>
> *And recognizing that life itself is a gift, and a call to responsibility, joy, and celebration, I make the following declarations:*
>
> *1. I declare myself to be a world citizen.*
>
> *2. I commit myself to lead an ecologically sound life.*
>
> *3. I commit myself to lead a life of creative simplicity and to share my personal wealth with the world's poor.*
>
> *4. I commit myself to join with others in reshaping institutions in order to bring about a more just global society in which each person has full access to the needed resources for their physical, emotional, intellectual, and spiritual growth.*
>
> *5. I commit myself to occupational accountability, and in so doing I will seek to avoid the creation of products which cause harm to others.*
>
> *6. I affirm the gift of my body, and commit myself to its proper nourishment and physical well-being.*
>
> *7. I commit myself to examine continually my relations with others and to attempt to relate honestly, morally, and lovingly to those around me.*
>
> *8. I commit myself to personal renewal through prayer, meditation, and study.*
>
> *9. I commit myself to responsible participation in a community of faith.*[12]

Their list begins and ends with the two most important parts: commitment as a world citizen to a community of faith. Our Holy Communion does the same thing. Within this community of faith we are placed in solidarity with the world. Amen.

Silence And The
Blessing Of God

God pity us and bless us,
 your face shine upon us,
that your ways be known in the earth,
 your deliverance by all the nations.
— *Psalm 67:1-2*

 The grace of the Lord Jesus Christ, and the
love of God, and the fellowhsip of the Holy
Spirit be with you all.
— *2 Corinthians 13:14*

For two months we have been using our sermons to talk about our *Rituals of Redemption*. Not only have we been sharing some of the history behind our liturgical ceremonies and explaining the necessary technique for performing these rituals, but we have also been trying to expose the connection between these worship traditions and our everyday living. The idea behind it all is that the way we maneuver our bodies, whether we are standing or kneeling or sitting, whether we are gesturing or bowing . . . . The idea is that when we get our bodies in on the action then our real selves are more involved in our worship.

Think of the rituals we have considered: When we make the Sign of the Cross we are remembering our baptisms, and together they give us a positive sense of identity and self-worth. When we kneel or bow, especially when we are confessing our sins, we are fostering a sense of honesty and integrity in our lives. When we read the Holy Gospel and preach its good news we are countering the bad news which infects so much of modern life. When we make music and sing our hymns we are adding to the sum total of beauty in our world.

When we burn incense to accompany our prayers we are practicing a necessary kind of introspection and reflection. When we turn to each other and share the peace of the Lord we are strengthening our sense of mutual fellowship and fostering a feeling of "family" within our parish. When we give sacrificial gifts of money and present them as our offerings we are committing ourselves to some worthy purpose outside of ourselves. When we share the Holy Communion, particularly with the symbol of the common chalice, we are putting ourselves in solidarity with each other, and in fact we are placed in solidarity with the world.

All of these symbolic ceremonies help us experience the love of God in Christ Jesus; they enable us to feel the freeing and redeeming work of his Holy Spirit. Which is why we are calling them our *Rituals of Redemption*.

It is fitting that on the Festival of Christ the King, the last Sunday in our church's year, we consider the last of these *Rituals of Redemption*: the keeping of silence, and the receiving of the Blessing.

We Lutherans have not been very good at either one of these. There are some monastic orders, such as the Trappists or Cistercians of the Strict Order, who thrive on a practice of basic austerities: perpetual silence; total abstinence from meat, fish and eggs; sleeping on straw mattresses on plank beds in common dormitories; rising at 2 a.m. to pray the Night Office; a regular diet of hard manual labor; that sort of thing. But we Lutherans, with our emphasis on preaching the Word and singing those hymns, have not been very big on silence.

And we are not much better with blessings. Oh, we know how to end our services with the Blessing or the Benediction, all right. But sometimes you get the idea that it functions as a way of saying, "Okay, it's all over; you can go home now." The idea that this is "an authoritative declaration of divine favor addressed to persons," as my liturgical dictionary puts it, sometimes gets lost in the shuffle as people are putting on their coats and readying the children to hustle them out the aisle.

And the idea of blessing something other than people —
a new home, for example, or new worship furnishings — nearly
borders on the superstitious for some of us. Have I told you
the story about a young woman who saved her money and then
bought a new Ferrari? She wanted it to be safe and protected,
so she went to her neighborhood Catholic church and asked
the priest, "Father, would you bless my Ferrari?" "I'll be
happy to, my daughter," he replied; "but what's a Ferrari?"

"Well, never mind," she said. Then she drove to the Epis-
copal rectory and asked, "Reverend, would you bless my Ferrari?" "Of course, my dear," he said; "but what's a Ferrari?"
Again she left disappointed. This time she came to the Lutheran
church. "Pastor," she asked, "would you please bless my Ferrari?" "I'd be delighted to do that," he answered; "but what's
a blessing?"

We have not always been entirely clear about what is happening when the minister pronounces a blessing, whether over
some object or even over ourselves, any more than we have
been clear about the role of silence in our worship.

Interestingly, there is one place in our service where these
two are joined. At the end of each celebration of the Holy
Communion we are invited to keep a time of "silence for reflection," and then "the minister blesses the congregation." Silence and the blessing of God are the last of our *Rituals of
Redemption* right before we are dismissed to carry our service into the world. So let's consider them separately, and then
we will bring them together to learn how silence and the blessing
of God affect our basic stance as people living in this world.

First, silence. I know many of you appreciate the chance
to arrive early for church and sit in quiet here in the sanctuary. The light through the stained glass, the vaulted Gothic
arches, the quiet decorum of those who are preparing the altar — you appreciate that silent time and the feeling of refuge
you enjoy at least for a few minutes each week. You are grateful
that those who want to visit confine their louder conversation
to the narthex and the hallways and the lounges. Such times
of silence are rare and cherished.

71

But there are other times, as part of our worship, when it is equally good for us to observe times of silence. During the occasional services of Matins and Vespers and Compline times of silence are to be kept after the praying of the psalms and the reading of each Lesson. Such quiet gives us opportunity to reflect on the biblical words we have just shared and to meditate on what they mean for our lives.

Such quiet times are not intended to be mere "moments of silence." They are to be long enough, at least a full minute or two, for us to compose our thoughts and set our minds at rest and give attention to those things which are truly important. This is not always easy, I know. It may take a while for us to stifle our last cough and for the children to quit kicking the pew. But it is worth the wait.

The minister's manual for our book of worship approaches the matter realistically:

> Introducing silence to a congregation requires some instruction. The people must know what to expect; otherwise, it may appear that someone has missed a cue. Unpracticed congregations require some time to begin to make use of the silence creatively.
>
> In a silence of two minutes, the first minute may be spent in restlessness, coughing, shuffling in the pews. Then, when the people settle down, the silence may be considered to have begun.
>
> Most people will welcome a time of quiet; such times are not easily found in a busy world. Neither music (not even soft organ music) nor the movement of leaders should intrude. All . . . sit in quiet meditation.[13]

In our regular Communion liturgy there are three places where we are to keep this kind of silence. The first is during the Brief Order for Confession and Forgiveness. As soon as we kneel, but before we actually begin to speak our confession, we are to observe a time of "silence for reflection and self-examination."

Our directions say that this "silence should be kept long enough for individual reflection and preparation, enabling personal application of the general phrases of the prayer to follow."[14] In other words, if we are going to confess before God our bondage to sin, the wrong we have done and the good left undone, and our lapses of love, it is right for us to think about what that really means. And without the quiet time to think, it is nearly impossible for our confession to be either real or honest.

Then again, right before the Prayer of the Day we may keep a brief silence. This gives us time to collect our thoughts before we begin this brief prayer. You know, in our older hymnals this prayer was known as the "Collect for the Day" because in a few brief phrases it collected the thoughts of the church for that particular liturgical occasion. We can retain some of that "collect" idea when we pause briefly to collect our thoughts.

Finally, as we said, we may observe "silence for reflection" after the prayer of thanksgiving for the Holy Communion, right before we hear the final Blessing. This briefer silence gives us a chance to review our worship and anticipate what it will mean for our living the rest of the week.

You have heard it said that "silence is golden." And so it is, especially when it is part of our worship. For such silence is not merely the absence of extraneous noise and distraction. It is of positive value. It takes some effort to use such silence for meaningful meditation and self-examination and reflection.

Interestingly, this kind of what we might call "active silence" seems to work better when we are doing it together. You would think it might be the other way around, that our best silence occurs when we are alone, by ourselves, away from any other potentially disturbing presence. But not so. When there are a hundred or two hundred or three hundred people together, all keeping silence, that is when the Spirit seems to stir quietly in our midst. That is when we feel the profound depth of our faith.

Such is silence. Now, secondly, the Blessing. We used to call this the Bendiction, which means to "speak well." The important thing to remember is that this is not merely a pious wish on the part of the speaker. But it is an objective announcement of God's own declaration about us.

I know there is a whole genre of so-called "blessings" that are fun to share on occasion: "May the road rise to meet you," and so forth. "May you be in heaven a half hour before the devil knows you're dead," and the like. But those are really pious or humorous wishes. What we are dealing with here is a real honest-to-God blessing, the objective announcement of God's own declaration to us and about us.

It goes back to Old Testament times, to the way the Lord God treated the people of Israel when he had rescued them from Egypt. Buried in the book of Numbers, mixed in with the laws for lepers and adulterers and Nazarite vows and gifts for the tabernacle, we are told that the Lord instructed Moses, who in turn was to instruct his brother Aaron the priest, about the ritual for blessing the people:

"You shall say to them: Yahweh bless you and keep you; Yahweh make his face to shine upon you," and so forth. You know the rest of the formula. The interesting part is the conclusion: "So shall they put my name upon the people of Israel," says the Lord God Yahweh, "and I will bless them." (Numbers 6:27) In other words, it is an accomplished fact.

When God's ministers speak the words, we are to consider ourselves blessed by God himself. No two ways about it; it's done, it's there, it's for us, and it's for good.

Centuries later the psalmist had that in mind when he composed the poem we chanted earlier. "God pity us and bless us," we sang, "your face shine upon us, that your ways be known in the earth, your deliverance by all the nations." The poet knew that if God's blessing rests on his people, that is an objective reality, something that can be seen and acknowledged by the rest of the world.

More centuries later the apostle St. Paul revised the formula. He had come to learn that the best of God's blessings come through his son, Jesus the Christ, and that those blessings are distributed through the power of his Holy Spirit. So when he wrote to his struggling church at Corinth he polished off his correspondence with this blessing: "The grace of the Lord Jesus Christ, and the love of God, and the fellowship of the Holy Spirit be with you all."

Now whenever the minister pronounces either of those blessings over us (or like today when we shall speak both of them), we receive it gratefully, under the Sign of the Cross, because we know that this is for real.

You see, when our brother Jesus was hanged up on that cross until he was dead, you would have thought that would have been the end of it all. And it should have been. Execution by crucifixion was calculated to extract the most excruciating pain, to inflict the most inhumane ignominy imaginable upon a human being. Strung up there naked and exposed, people could sometimes last two, three, four or more days before death rattled in their throats and they went limp and cold. Often victims of this ultimate torture were reduced to demented cursing and enraged madness.

But something else was going on when they strung up Jesus, something royal, something kingly, some benefaction. So when that other sniveling bandit finally acknowledged it, he received the ultimate blessing. "Remember me," he asked, "when you come into your kingdom." "Today," he was promised. "Today you will be with me in paradise." (Luke 23:43)

In silence we would receive such a benediction. And having received it, everything would look different. The whole universe would be altered. We would know exactly where we stand in the eternal scheme of things, where we stand before God. We would be put right in our places, sliced down to proper size. And then we would be more exalted than we dared ever hope.

Our classic Lutheran dogmatics texts sometimes used a pair of Latin phrases that caught this idea. One was *coram Deo*; another was *sub specie aeternitatis*. The one means "in the presence of God"; the other means "under the perspective of eternity." They are reminders that we do not live out our four score years and ten under our own authority. We do not run the world; the world runs us. Oftentimes what we inhabit is a chance and random universe.

When Rabbi Kuschner wrote his book, *When Bad Things Happen to Good People*, he saw clearly how necessary it is for us to acknowledge that we live in a random universe, in which bad things sometimes just happen. It's nobody's fault; it's just the luck of the draw.

And when "the big quake of '89" rattled San Francisco, time and again people said how it made them realize how out of control we really are, how nothing can be taken for granted. That, folks, is part of what we mean by living "under the perspective of eternity." We live "before God" exposed and vulnerable.

But side by side with that harsh reality is a saving word, a benediction the pronouncement of which changes our eternal perspective of life before God. It is God's own declaration that blesses us and so makes us blessed. Because it is not our own devising, we can only accept it in silence.

That, Brothers and Sisters, is the new redemptive reality in which we now live. It changes everything about the way we look at the world. It is silence, and the blessing of God. Amen.

Notes

1. Jonathan Z. Smith, "The Bare Facts of Ritual," *Imagining Religion* (Univeristy of Chicago, 1982) p. 54.

2. *The Lutheran Hymnal* (St. Louis: Concordia, 1941) p. 4.

3. *The New Westminster Dictionary of Liturgy and Worship* (ed. J.G. Davies; Philadelphia: Westminster, 1986) p. 384.

4. *Lutheran Book of Worship* (Minneapolis: Augsburg, 1978) no. 544.

5 . *Lutheran Book of Worship: Minister's Desk Edition* (Minneapolis: Augsburg, 1978) p. 38.

6. *Luther's Works: Liturgy and Hymns* (ed. Ulrich Lupold; Philadelphia: Fortress, 1965) vol. 53, p. 25.

7. *Luther's Works: Lectures on Genesis* (ed. Paul D. Pahl; St. Louis: Concordia, 1965) vol. 7, p. 135.

8. *Lutheran Book of Worship: Minister's Desk Edition*, p. 38.

9. William R. White, *Stories for the Journey* (Minneapolis: Augsburg, 1988) p. 97.

10. Paul H. D. Lang, *Ceremony and Celebration* (St. Louis: Concordia, 1965) p. 98.

11. "The Augsburg Confession, Article 22," *The Book of Concord* (ed. Theodore Tappert; Philadelphia: Muhlenberg, 1959) p. 49.

12. George S. Johnson, *Beyond Guilt and Powerlessness* (Minneapolis: Augsburg-Fortress, 1989) p. 95.

13. Philip H. Pfatteicher and Charles R. Messerli, *Manual on the Liturgy: Lutheran Book of Worship* (Minneapolis: Augsburg, 1979) p. 259.

14. *Lutheran Book of Worship: Minister's Desk Edition*, p. 26.